Becoming a Dragonfly

by Grace Hansen

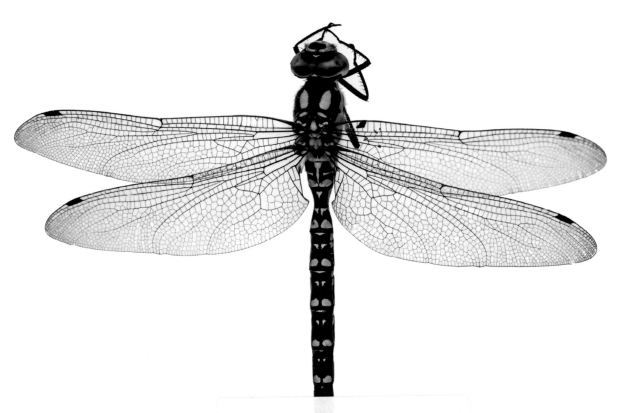

Abdo
CHANGING ANIMALS
Kids

abdopublishing.com

Published by Abdo Kids, a division of ABDO, PO Box 398166, Minneapolis, Minnesota 55439.

Copyright © 2017 by Abdo Consulting Group, Inc. International copyrights reserved in all countries.
No part of this book may be reproduced in any form without written permission from the publisher.

Printed in the United States of America, North Mankato, Minnesota.

052016

092016

 THIS BOOK CONTAINS RECYCLED MATERIALS

Photo Credits: iStock, Minden Pictures, Shutterstock

Production Contributors: Teddy Borth, Jennie Forsberg, Grace Hansen

Design Contributors: Laura Mitchell, Dorothy Toth

Cataloging-in-Publication Data

Names: Hansen, Grace, author.

Title: Becoming a dragonfly / by Grace Hansen.

Description: Minneapolis, MN : Abdo Kids, [2017] | Series: Changing animals |
    Includes bibliographical references and index.

Identifiers: LCCN 2015959109 | ISBN 9781680805086 (lib. bdg.) |
    ISBN 9781680805642 (ebook) | ISBN 9781680806205 (Read-to-me ebook)

Subjects: LCSH: Dragonflies--Juvenile literature. | Life cycles--Juvenile literature.

Classification: DDC 595.7--dc23

LC record available at http://lccn.loc.gov/2015959109

Table of Contents

Stage 1

All dragonflies begin as eggs. Dragonflies lay their eggs in water.

4

Stage 2

A dragonfly hatches from its egg after two or three weeks. But it does not look like a dragonfly at all! It is in its **larval** stage.

A dragonfly **larva** is called a **nymph**. It has six legs and two large eyes. It also has **gills**. It can breathe underwater.

9

Stage 3

The **nymph** is a good hunter. It eats other insects. It even eats small fish and tadpoles! It eats and grows. It **molts** as it grows.

The **nymph** is full-grown after one or two years. It leaves the water. It is ready to become a dragonfly.

Stage 4

The **nymph** finds a dry and safe place. The dragonfly pushes itself out of its nymph skin. First its head **emerges**, followed by its **thorax**.

15

The dragonfly is halfway out. It takes a break. It hangs and waits for its legs to harden. Then, it reaches up and grabs its old body. It pulls the rest of its body out!

The dragonfly's wings expand.
It takes about an hour for them
to dry. The dragonfly is pale
green. After a week, it will have
its adult colors and patterns.

19

If it is lucky, the dragonfly will live about six to eight weeks. In that time, it will find a **mate**.

21

More Facts

- Dragonflies live near calm freshwater, like rivers, streams, lakes, and ponds.

- Dragonflies rely very much on water. Their numbers let us know how healthy our freshwater is. If there are very few dragonflies in an area, water quality might be bad. If there are lots, the water is good!

- Dragonflies are great fliers. They can fly in any direction, and can even hover in one place.

Glossary

emerge – to come into view.

gill – an organ of aquatic animals that breathe oxygen in water.

larva – an active immature form of an insect.

mate – one of a pair of animals that will have young together.

molt – to shed skin that will be replaced by new skin.

nymph – a young insect that has almost the same form as the adult.

thorax – the portion of the body between the head and the abdomen.

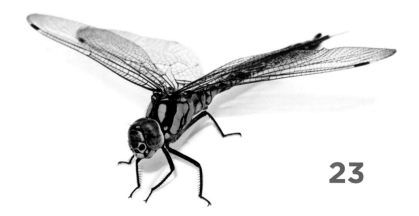

Index

abdokids.com

Use this code to log on to abdokids.com and access crafts, games, videos, and more!

Abdo Kids Code:
CBK5086